THE NEW FOOD GUIDE PYRAMID

Fruits

by Emily K. Green

BLASTOFF!
2
READERS

BELLWETHER MEDIA · MINNEAPOLIS, MN

Note to Librarians, Teachers, and Parents:

Blastoff! Readers are carefully developed by literacy experts and combine standards-based content with developmentally appropriate text.

Level 1 provides the most support through repetition of high-frequency words, light text, predictable sentence patterns, and strong visual support.

Level 2 offers early readers a bit more challenge through varied simple sentences, increased text load, and less repetition of high-frequency words.

Level 3 advances early-fluent readers toward fluency through increased text and concept load, less reliance on visuals, longer sentences, and more literary language.

Whichever book is right for your reader, Blastoff! Readers are the perfect books to build confidence and encourage a love of reading that will last a lifetime!

This edition first published in 2007 by Bellwether Media.

No part of this publication may be reproduced in whole or in part without written permission of the publisher. For information regarding permission, write to Bellwether Media Inc., Attention: Permissions Department, Post Office Box 1C, Minnetonka, MN 55345-9998.

Library of Congress Cataloging-in-Publication Data

Green, Emily K., 1966-
 Fruits / by Emily K. Green.
    p. cm. — (Blastoff! readers) (New food guide pyramid)
Summary: "A basic introduction to the health benefits of fruits. Intended for kindergarten through third grade students."
 Includes bibliographical references and index.
 ISBN-10: 1-60014-005-X (hardcover : alk. paper)
 ISBN-13: 978-1-60014-005-1
 1. Fruit in human nutrition—Juvenile literature. 2. Nutrition—Juvenile literature. I. Title. II. Series.

QP144.F78G74 2007
613.2—dc22   2006000409

Table of Contents

Kids need to eat healthy
foods every day.

4

The **food guide pyramid** can help you choose healthy foods.

Grains

Vegetables

Each color stripe on the
pyramid stands for a
food group.

6

The Food Guide Pyramid

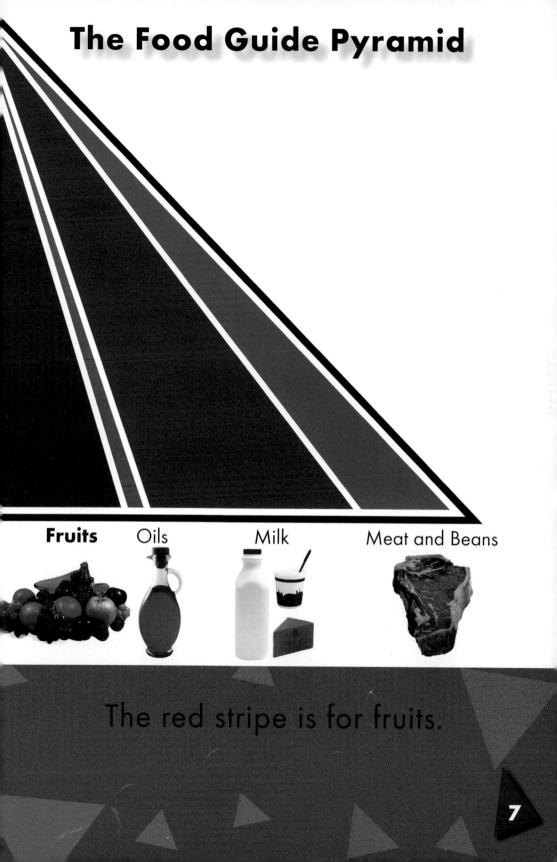

Fruits   Oils   Milk   Meat and Beans

The red stripe is for fruits.

Strawberries, apples, kiwis, and lemons are in the fruits group.

Blueberries are in the
fruits group.

9

Fruit has **vitamin C**. Vitamin C helps make your teeth and bones strong.

Vitamin C also helps your body fight colds and heal cuts.

Fruits give you **energy** to play and learn.

Fruits have **fiber**. Fiber helps food move through your body.

Fruits are **naturally** sweet and low in **calories**.

Eating snacks that are low in calories can help you keep a healthy weight.

1 ½ cups

1 large apple = 1 ½ cups

Kids should eat about one and a half cups of fruit each day.

12 strawberries = 1½ cups

There are many kinds of fruit. You can eat different colored fruits every day.

Reach for fruits when you want something sweet.

Fruits are fun to eat.

How Much Should A Kid Eat Each Day?

Vegetables
2½ cups

Fruits
1½ cups

Grains
6 servings

Oils
5 teaspoons

Milk, Yogurt, and Cheese
3 cups

Meat and Beans
1-2 servings

21

Glossary

calories—a unit that measures how much energy food gives your body

energy—the power to move

fiber—the part of a plant that stays whole when it moves through your body

food guide pyramid—a chart showing the kinds and amounts of foods you should eat each day

naturally—the way that something is in nature; something that is naturally sweet has not had any extra sugar added.

vitamin C—a part of some foods that helps to keep your teeth and bones strong

To Learn More

AT THE LIBRARY

French, Vivian. *Oliver's Fruit Salad*. New York: Orchard Books, 1998.

Gibbons, Gail. *The Berry Book*. New York: Holiday House, 2002.

Marzollo, Jean. *I Am an Apple*. New York: Scholastic, 1997.

Rockwell, Lizzy. *Good Enough to Eat: A Kid's Guide To Food And Nutrition*. New York: HarperCollins, 1999.

ON THE WEB
Learning more about healthy eating is as easy as 1, 2, 3.

1. Go to www.factsurfer.com

2. Enter "healthy eating" into search box.

3. Click the "Surf" button and you will see a list of related web sites.

With factsurfer.com, finding more information is just a click away.

Index

The photographs in this book are reproduced through the courtesy of: Susan Kinast/Food Pix, front cover; Christina Kennedy/Getty Images, pp. 4-5, 18-19; Michael S Quinton/Getty Images, p. 6-7; Paul Webster/Getty Images, p. 8; Michael Skott/Getty Images, p. 9; Wizdata, Inc., p. 10; Donn Thompson/Getty Images, p. 11; Shannon Fagan/Getty Images, p. 12; Robin MacDougall/Getty Images, p. 13; Michael Brauner/Getty Images, pp. 14-15; davies & starr/Getty Images, p. 16; Jostein Hauge, p. 17; Juan Martinez, p. 20(top); Tim McClellan, p. 20(middle, bottom), p. 21 (bottom); Michael Rosenfeld/Getty Images, p. 21(top); Olga Lyubkina, p. 21(middle).